Comptroller of the Currency
Administrator of National Banks

I0448525

Management Information Systems

Comptroller's Handbook

May 1995

Management

Management
Information Systems
Table of Contents

Management
Information Systems Introduction

Background

A management information system (MIS) is a system or process that provides the information necessary to manage an organization effectively. MIS and the information it generates are generally considered essential components of prudent and reasonable business decisions.

The importance of maintaining a consistent approach to the development, use, and review of MIS systems within the institution must be an ongoing concern of both bank management and OCC examiners. MIS should have a clearly defined framework of guidelines, policies or practices, standards, and procedures for the organization. These should be followed throughout the institution in the development, maintenance, and use of all MIS.

MIS is viewed and used at many levels by management. It should be supportive of the institution's longer term strategic goals and objectives. To the other extreme it is also those everyday financial accounting systems that are used to ensure basic control is maintained over financial recordkeeping activities.

Financial accounting systems and subsystems are just one type of institutional MIS. Financial accounting systems are an important functional element or part of the total MIS structure. However, they are more narrowly focused on the internal balancing of an institution's books to the general ledger and other financial accounting subsystems. For example, accrual adjustments, reconciling and correcting entries used to reconcile the financial systems to the general ledger are not always immediately entered into other MIS systems. Accordingly, although MIS and accounting reconcilement totals for related listings and activities should be similar, they may not necessarily balance.

An institution's MIS should be designed to achieve the following goals:

- Enhance communication among employees.
- Deliver complex material throughout the institution.
- Provide an objective system for recording and aggregating information.

- Reduce expenses related to labor-intensive manual activities.
- Support the organization's strategic goals and direction.

Because MIS supplies decision makers with facts, it supports and enhances the overall decision making process. MIS also enhances job performance throughout an institution. At the most senior levels, it provides the data and information to help the board and management make strategic decisions. At other levels, MIS provides the means through which the institution's activities are monitored and information is distributed to management, employees, and customers.

Effective MIS should ensure the appropriate presentation formats and time frames required by operations and senior management are met. MIS can be maintained and developed by either manual or automated systems or a combination of both. It should always be sufficient to meet an institution's unique business goals and objectives. The effective deliveries of an institution's products and services are supported by the MIS. These systems should be accessible and useable at all appropriate levels of the organization.

MIS is a critical component of the institution's overall risk management strategy. MIS supports management's ability to perform such reviews. MIS should be used to recognize, monitor, measure, limit, and manage risks. Risk management involves four main elements:

- Policies or practices.
- Operational processes.
- Staff and management.
- Feedback devices.

Frequently, operational processes and feedback devices are intertwined and cannot easily be viewed separately. The most efficient and useable MIS should be both operational and informational. As such, management can use MIS to measure performance, manage resources, and help an institution comply with regulatory requirements. One example of this would be the managing and reporting of loans to insiders. MIS can also be used by management to provide feedback on the effectiveness of risk controls. Controls are developed to support the proper management of risk through the institution's policies or practices, operational processes, and the assignment of duties and responsibilities to staff and managers.

Technology advances have increased both the availability and volume of information management and the directors have available for both planning and decision making. Correspondingly, technology also increases the potential for inaccurate reporting and flawed decision making. Because data can be extracted from many financial and transaction systems, appropriate control procedures must be set up to ensure that information is correct and relevant. In addition, since MIS often originates from multiple equipment platforms including mainframes, minicomputers, and microcomputers, controls must ensure that systems on smaller computers have processing controls that are as well defined and as effective as those commonly found on the traditionally larger mainframe systems.

All institutions must set up a framework of sound fundamental principles that identify risk, establish controls, and provide for effective MIS review and monitoring systems throughout the organization. Commonly, an organization may choose to establish and express these sound principles in writing. The OCC fully endorses and supports placing these principles in writing to enhance effective communications throughout the institution. If however, management follows sound fundamental principles and governs the risk in the MIS Review area, a written policy is not required by the OCC. If sound principles are not effectively practiced, the OCC may require management to establish written MIS policies to formally communicate risk parameters and controls in this area.

Sound fundamental principles for MIS review include proper internal controls, operating procedures and safeguards, and audit coverage. These principles are explained throughout this booklet.

Risks Associated With MIS

Risk reflects the potential, the likelihood, or the expectation of events that could adversely affect earnings or capital. Management uses MIS to help in the assessment of risk within an institution. Management decisions based upon ineffective, inaccurate, or incomplete MIS may increase risk in a number of areas such as credit quality, liquidity, market/pricing, interest rate, or foreign currency. A flawed MIS causes operational risks and can adversely affect an organization's monitoring of its fiduciary, consumer, fair lending, Bank Secrecy Act, or other compliance-related activities.

Since management requires information to assess and monitor performance at all levels of the organization, MIS risk can extend to all levels of the operations. Additionally, poorly programmed or non-secure systems in which data can be manipulated and/or systems requiring ongoing repairs can easily disrupt routine work flow and can lead to incorrect decisions or impaired planning.

Assessing Vulnerability To MIS Risk

To function effectively as an interacting, interrelated, and interdependent feedback tool for management and staff, MIS must be "useable." The five elements of a useable MIS system are: timeliness, accuracy, consistency, completeness, and relevance. The usefulness of MIS is hindered whenever one or more of these elements is compromised.

Timeliness

To simplify prompt decision making, an institution's MIS should be capable of providing and distributing current information to appropriate users. Information systems should be designed to expedite reporting of information. The system should be able to quickly collect and edit data, summarize results, and be able to adjust and correct errors promptly.

Accuracy

A sound system of automated and manual internal controls must exist throughout all information systems processing activities. Information should receive appropriate editing, balancing, and internal control checks. A comprehensive internal and external audit program should be employed to ensure the adequacy of internal controls.

Consistency

To be reliable, data should be processed and compiled consistently and uniformly. Variations in how data is collected and reported can distort information and trend analysis. In addition, because data collection and reporting processes will change over time, management must establish sound procedures to allow for systems changes. These procedures should be well defined and documented, clearly communicated to appropriate employees, and should include an effective monitoring system.

Completeness

Decision makers need complete and pertinent information in a summarized form. Reports should be designed to eliminate clutter and voluminous detail, thereby avoiding "information overload."

Relevance

Information provided to management must be relevant. Information that is inappropriate, unnecessary, or too detailed for effective decision making has no value. MIS must be appropriate to support the management level using it. The relevance and level of detail provided through MIS systems directly correlate to what is needed by the board of directors, executive management, departmental or area mid-level managers, etc. in the performance of their jobs.

Achieving Sound MIS

The development of sound MIS is the result of the development and enforcement of a culture of system ownership. An "owner" is a system user who knows current customer and constituent needs and also has budget authority to fund new projects. Building "ownership" promotes pride in institution processes and helps ensure accountability.

Although MIS does not necessarily reduce expenses, the development of meaningful systems, and their proper use, will lessen the probability that erroneous decisions will be made because of inaccurate or untimely information. Erroneous decisions invariably misallocate and/or waste resources. This may result in an adverse impact on earnings and/or capital.

MIS which meets the five elements of useability is a critical ingredient to an institution's short- and long-range planning efforts. To achieve sound MIS, the organization's planning process should include consideration of MIS needs at both the tactical and strategic levels. For example, at a tactical level MIS systems and report output should support the annual operating plan and budgetary processes. They should also be used in support of the long term strategic MIS and business planning initiatives. Without the development of an effective MIS, it is more difficult for management to measure and monitor the success of new initiatives and the progress of ongoing projects. Two common examples of this would be the management of mergers and acquisitions or the continuing development and the introduction of new products and services.

Management needs to ensure that MIS systems are developed according to a sound methodology that encompasses the following phases:

- Appropriate analysis of system alternatives, approval points as the system is developed or acquired, and task organization.
- Program development and negotiation of contracts with equipment and software vendors.
- Development of user instructions, training, and testing of the system.
- Installation and maintenance of the system.

Management should also consider use of "project management techniques" to monitor progress as the MIS system is being developed. Internal controls must be woven into the processes and periodically reviewed by auditors.

Management also should ensure that managers and staff receive initial and ongoing training in MIS. In addition, user manuals should be available and provide the following information:

- A brief description of the application or system.
- Input instructions, including collection points and times to send updated information.
- Balancing and reconciliation procedures.
- A complete listing of output reports, including samples.

Depending on the size and complexity of its MIS system, an institution may need to use different manuals for different users such as first-level users, unit managers, and programmers.

MIS Reviews

By its very nature, management information is designed to meet the unique needs of individual institutions. As a result, MIS requirements will vary depending on the size and complexity of the operations. For example, systems suitable for community sized institutions will not necessarily be adequate for larger institutions. However, basic information needs or requirements are similar in all financial institutions regardless of size. The complexity of the operations and/or activities, together with institution size, point to the need for MIS of varying degrees of complexity to support the decision-making processes. Examiners should base MIS reviews on an evaluation of whether the system(s) provide management and directors with the information necessary to guide operations, support timely decision making, and help management monitor progress toward reaching institutional goals and objectives. Although examiners should encourage management to develop sound information systems, they also should be reasonable in their expectations about what constitutes suitable MIS.

Examiner MIS reviews are normally focused on a specific area of activity, on a clearly identifiable departmental or functional basis, or as a part of the activity being examined within a larger department.

During the examination, the MIS review should occur at both a macro (big picture) level and also at the micro (functional/product oriented view of the business) level. The examiner-in-charge of the MIS-review program should look at the useability and effectiveness of the corporate-wide MIS structure. The examiner should also collect MIS related observations and information from the examiners-in-charge of the other areas under review. It would be very difficult for one examiner to attempt to perform a detailed MIS review for all of an organization's functional and operational areas of activity. It is practical and reasonable, however, to have this lead examiner coordinate and consolidate the MIS reviews from the other examination areas. The MIS related feedback received from other area examiners provides important and practical input to the MIS review examiner. The consolidation, coordination, and analysis of this MIS feedback can be used to reach supportable macro-level conclusions and recommendations for corporate-wide MIS activities.

MIS reviews in the functional or product review areas generally should be performed by an examiner who is considered to be a subject matter expert (SME) in the area of activities or operations that are being supported by the MIS systems or processes under review. The SME must have a thorough and complete understanding of the baseline "business" supported by the MIS system(s) under review. A solid understanding of the business is fundamental to the completion of a meaningful MIS review. The decision regarding the overall quality and effectiveness of MIS generally should be made by the SME for the area under review. The SME for each area where MIS is under review must subsequently communicate MIS related findings, conclusions, and opinions to the examiner charged with the responsibility for the complete MIS review work program at that examination. This is clearly a collaborative effort among area SMEs and the examiner charged with the responsibility for this area of review.

The examiner coordinating the overall MIS review program should be a commercial examiner with broad experience and understanding which covers many areas of organizational operations and activity. Alternatively, a bank information systems (BIS) examiner could serve in this capacity. BIS examiners should be consulted whenever there are questions, issues, or concerns surrounding the use of information systems (IS) or electronic data processing (EDP) technology or the effectiveness of MIS-related internal controls in any automated area of the organization's activities.

When performing MIS reviews, examiners should use the guidelines in this booklet to determine if management has:

- Identified the institution's specific information requirements. Examiners can focus on specific information needs related to issues such as asset quality, interest rate risk, regulatory reporting, and compliance. If possible, the MIS review should be concurrent with examinations of the commercial, consumer, fiduciary, and BIS activities. This would enhance interaction and communication among examiners.

- Established effective reporting mechanisms to guide decisions. This process includes reviewing controls that ensure that information is reliable, timely, accurate, and confidential.

1.	To determine examination procedures necessary to achieve stated objectives. (Note: BIS examiner support of commercial staff should be considered to enhance the depth of coverage for the MIS review if there are known MIS issues or deficiencies which represent an undue level of risk and/or if MIS activities are particularly complex or sophisticated.)

2.	To determine if MIS policies or practices, processes, objectives, and internal controls are adequate.

3.	To evaluate whether MIS applications provide users with timely, accurate, consistent, complete, and relevant information.

4.	To assess the types and level of risk associated with MIS and the quality of controls over those risks.

5.	To determine whether MIS applications and enhancements to existing systems adequately support corporate goals.

6.	To determine if MIS is being developed in compliance with an approved corporate MIS policy or practice statement.

7.	To determine if management is committed to providing the resources needed to develop the required MIS.

8.	To determine if officers are operating according to established guidelines.

9.	To evaluate the scope and adequacy of audit activities.

10.	To initiate corrective action when policies or practices, processes, objectives, or internal controls are deficient.

11.	To determine if any additional work is needed to fulfill the examination strategy of the institution.

1.   Obtain the following documents:

         ☐   Examination Report and related management responses.
         ☐   Supervisory Monitoring System (SMS) comments.
         ☐   MIS-related workpapers.
         ☐   MIS-related audit/compliance reviews.
         ☐   Institution's formal MIS policies and practices framework/guidelines.
         ☐   Board/MIS Committee-related minutes.
         ☐   Organization charts detailing MIS responsibility.

2.   Review previous MIS review-related examination findings. Review management's response to those findings.

         •   Discuss with OCC examiners their perception of both the usefulness and applicability of the five MIS elements applicable to MIS systems that have been reviewed or are pending review.
         •   Request copies of any reports which discuss either MIS deficiencies or strengths from the SME examiners.
         •   Determine the significance of deficiencies and set priorities for follow-up investigations.

3.   Request and review copies of recent reports prepared by internal or external auditors of targeted MIS area(s). Determine the following:

         •   The significance of MIS problems disclosed.
         •   Recommendations provided for resolving MIS deficiencies.
         •   Management's responses and whether corrective actions have been initiated and/or completed.
         •   Audit follow-up activities.

4.   Review the Supervisory Strategy in the Supervisory Monitoring System and Scope Memorandum issued by the examiner-in-charge (EIC).

5.   Review reports for the MIS target area(s). Determine any material changes involving the usefulness of information and the five MIS elements:

- Timeliness.
- Accuracy.
- Consistency.
- Completeness.
- Relevance.

6. Review MIS-related policies or practices and processes. Pay special attention to any changes since the previous review.

7. Review the Internal Control Questionnaire (ICQ) and determine which questions and/or sections should be used to support the examination's MIS review.

8. Based on the performance of the previous steps, and discussions with the EIC and other appropriate supervisors, determine the scope of the examination and set the objectives.

Select from among the following examination procedures those steps that are necessary to meet the objectives. Examinations may not require all of the steps.

9. In conjunction with the EIC, identify each of the functional or product-related areas to be reviewed at this examination. Once the scope of the MIS review has been determined:

- Provide copies of the MIS objectives, ICQs, and examination procedures to the SME examiner(s). Highlight those areas of MIS review that need to be addressed during the review.

- The MIS review examiner will aggregate these observations, conclusions, and recommendations for each of the functional areas addressed and incorporate them (as appropriate) into the final MIS Review conclusions.

- If there are issues, observations, conclusions or recommendations related to operational or technology aspects of the institution's MIS, the commercial examiner should coordinate these with the BIS examiner or BIS manager if the BIS examiner is not already involved in the MIS review process.

10.   For the selected sample of MIS system(s) and as appropriate to support the defined scope, obtain:

☐   User manual.
☐   User training manual/instructions.
☐   Project plan and related workpapers.
☐   Sample of MIS Output Reports.
☐   MIS project development/enhancement workpapers.

11.   As examination procedures are performed, test for compliance with established policies or practices and processes, and the existence of appropriate internal control measures. Refer to the Internal Control Questionnaire as needed.

12.   Identify any area with inadequate supervision and/or undue risk. Discuss with the EIC the need to perform verification procedures. As required, perform appropriate verification procedures.

13.   Select and review samples of ongoing executive reports for the targeted MIS area(s). Determine whether:

•   The source of the information collected originates from the expected business area.
•   Users of the information are the appropriate employees or managers within that area of activity.
•   The reports are ultimately distributed to the appropriate users.
•   The flow of these MIS information/reports is consistent with the responsibilities reflected on the area's official organization chart.

14.   Determine the degree to which management and the staff in an area under review use MIS adequately and can support that the MIS being used is appropriate and effective. Perform the following steps:

•   Discuss the five MIS elements with a senior manager(s) of the respective business unit.
•   Repeat this work step with an employee of the business unit who has experience with the MIS system. (Note: This task is designed to determine if significant differences regarding the adequacy of the MIS exist among management and/or staff.)
•   Based on management's self-assessment of the useability of its

MIS, identify any planned activities to enhance, modify, or expand these systems.

15. Review minutes of the board of directors or committee(s) representing the MIS target area(s) for a relevant time period.

   - Determine any areas where the "packet" of information does not seem to meet the five required elements of MIS.
   - Identify MIS issues for follow up.

16. Request a copy of the development plan for significant MIS-related projects. Examples could include executive information packets, credit approval and take-out commitments, and funds management systems.

   - Review MIS project objectives and determine if they address reported MIS weaknesses and meet business unit plans.
   - Review the project management technique used by management and determine the status of important MIS projects.
   - Sample a significant MIS project(s) and determine whether it follows an approved and implemented development methodology that encompass the following phases:

) Analysis of system alternatives, organization of tasks, and approval of phases by system users/owners.
) Program development and negotiation of contracts for equipment and software vendors.
) Development of user instructions and system testing procedures.
) Installation and maintenance of the system.

17. Select a system and request copies of relevant user instructions. Determine whether the guidelines are meaningful, easy to understand, and current.

18. Determine whether user manuals provide adequate guidelines in the following areas:

   - Complete description of the system.
   - Input instructions, including collection points and times to sendupdated information.

- Balancing/reconciliation instructions.
- Full listing of output reports, including sample formats.

19. Obtain from the user manuals or the appropriate manager a work flow showing data from the point-of-entry, through user processes, to final product. The purpose of this task is to review how information is identified, gathered, merged, manipulated, and presented. (Depending on the organization's sophistication and system size, examiners may have to develop this work flow themselves.)

- Discuss the area's MIS process with a representative sample of users and determine if they know where the data is coming from, where it is going, and how it gets there. A complete understanding would suggest the interviewees both use and understand the MIS system(s) supporting them.
- Identify and note the points where adjustments to data occur.
- Identify the department staff who are responsible for the MIS-related input data and reports; i.e., obtain a list of users, ad hoc software report writers, and the programmers involved. Compare this information with the material acquired in the immediately preceding item.
- Determine if preparation and reconciliation processes are sufficient to reasonably ensure integrity of information.
- Determine if data adjustments are adequately documented.
- Determine the effectiveness of ad hoc report-writing capabilities by reviewing the software vendor's user manual for data presentations.
- Through observation and interview determine useability, commonality, simplicity, and effectiveness of MIS reports supporting the decision-making process for that area of activity.

20. Review the lines of communication within the institution and determine the effectiveness of MIS in the following areas:

- Communication paths linking executives, appropriate users, and information systems employees.
- The flow of communication throughout the organization.
- The documentation of which underlying MIS process supports the area's management.

21. Determine the adequacy of MIS training including whether:
     - Training needs are properly identified and prioritized.
     - Training is organized in a formal classroom setting, is on-the-job, or is a combination of both approaches.
     - Training manuals or other material besides the user manual exist.
     - The training material adequately covers relevant and current issues.
     - Training material is distributed to the appropriate employees.

22. Determine whether established procedures are sufficient to ensure the proper testing of system developments or enhancements.

23. Review whether final versions of software enhancements are installed in a controlled environment that promotes integrity of information.

24   Determine if authorized processes are followed as data is acquired, merged, manipulated, and up-loaded from subsystems.

25. Determine if the organization has had recent merger and/or acquisition activity. If it has, determine how management at the senior and departmental levels ensure that the resulting MIS supports and includes the five MIS elements mentioned previously. If mergers and acquisitions are frequent, determine whether:

     - Appropriate policies or practices and procedures have been developed to support such activity from an integrated MIS perspective.
     - The consolidation of MIS systems in a merger still meets the requirements of a quality MIS system.

26. Review the results of your work, summarize your findings and initial conclusions, and discuss issues with an appropriate officer(s):

     - How well risks are controlled.
     - Identify significant control deficiencies.
     - Recommend action to remove deficiencies.
     - Obtain management's corrective commitments and firm time frames.

---

27. Prepare a memorandum of your conclusions and supporting findings. Identify suggested OCC follow-up actions.

28. After a full discussion with the EIC prepare a memorandum and document work programs to facilitate future examinations.

Management
Information Systems   Internal Control Questionnaire

Purpose

The following questionnaire is provided as a tool to assist examiners in the assessment, review, and documentation of the quality of the bank's MIS-related internal controls, policies, practices, and procedures. However, because the nature and scope of MIS among banks, not all of the questions will be relevant in every bank. Similarly, a negative answer to a particular question does not necessarily indicate a weakness in the bank's MIS or surrounding internal controls if other equally effective or alternate controls are in place or there are other circumstances that mitigate the risk. Where appropriate, documentation may include narrative descriptions, flowcharts, copies of forms used, and substantiation through observation or testing.

Examiners should use their own judgement in deciding which internal control questions are relevant for a particular bank and whether a negative response to any particular question should be considered a matter of supervisory concern.

MIS Policies or Practices

Yes   No

1.   Has management developed and maintained a current
      MIS policy or practice?

2.   Does the policy or practice provide guidance in the
      following areas:

    •   The definition, purpose, and fundamental
         components of MIS?
    •   How to achieve effective two-way
         communication between management and
         employees and specific avenues to maintain such
         communication?
    •   Processes for initiating, developing, and
         completing MIS enhancements?
    •   Guidelines for installing MIS enhancements in a
         controlled change environment?

- Procedures for acquiring, merging, manipulating, and up-loading data to other systems?
- Guidance for delineating the need for internal/external audit coverage and testing?

3. Is the policy or practice reviewed and updated regularly?

4. Is the policy or practice distributed to appropriate employees?

5. Does the policy or practice incorporate or require:

- User approval for each phase?
- Installation of MIS enhancements in a controlled change environment?
- Employees to follow policy or practice and processes as data is acquired, merged, manipulated, and up-loaded to other systems?
- Employees to be sufficiently trained for new systems and subsequent enhancements?

MIS Development

6. Does the internal planning process consider and incorporate the importance of MIS at both the strategic and tactical level?

- Are longer term strategic goals (beyond 2 years) supported by the development of appropriate MIS?
- Are shorter term tactical goals over the immediate one-to-two year period regularly and appropriately reviewed and monitored by management?

7.   Do project objectives address reported MIS weaknesses and meet business unit requirements?

8.   Does management have a process for monitoring project schedules?

9.   Does management use a project management technique to monitor MIS development schedules?

10.   Does the organization use a consistent and standardized approach or a structured methodology for developing MIS projects?

11.   Does the methodology encompass the following phases:

- Analysis of the concept, organization of tasks, completions of phases, and approvals?
- Development of the program and contracting for equipment and software?
- Development of user manuals and testing of the system?
- Post-review of the system and future maintenance of it?

User Training and Instructions

12.   Is the user manual for the MIS system(s) meaningful, easy to understand, and current?

13.   Do user manual requirements include the following information:

- A brief description of the application or system?
- Input instructions, including collection points and times to send updated information?
- Balancing/reconciliation instructions?

- A full listing of output reports, including samples?

Communication

14. Does management encourage communication lines to meet the following objectives:

- To effectively link executives, other appropriate users, and information systems employees?
- To ensure effective two-way communication between management and employees?
- To document the MIS process?

Audit

15. Has the MIS target area(s) been internally or externally audited in the past two years?

- If it has, review the scope of the audit, the findings, and management's response(s) to that report.

- If it hasn't, interview audit management to determine what their plans regarding an audit review of the MIS system are.

Yes   No

Conclusion

16. Can this information be considered adequate for evaluating internal control of MIS activities? This question presumes that there are no additional significant internal auditing procedures, accounting controls, administrative controls, or other circumstances that impair any controls or mitigate any weaknesses noted above. (Note: Explain negative answers briefly, and indicate conclusions as to their effect on specific examination or verification procedures.)

17. Based on a composite evaluation, evidenced by answers to the previous questions, internal control is considered to be _____ (good, medium, or bad).

1. Using an appropriate sampling technique, select an additional MIS project(s) from the organization's development plan.

   - Review project objectives and determine if they address reported MIS weaknesses and meet business unit plans.
   - Determine whether the MIS projects follow an approved and implemented development methodology that encompass the following phases:

) Analysis of system alternatives, organization of tasks, and approval of phases by system users/owners.
) Program development and contracts for equipment and software vendors.
) Development of user instructions and testing the system changes.
) Installation and maintenance of the system.

2. Using the expanded sample, check copies of relevant user instructions. Verify whether the guidelines are meaningful, easy to understand, and current.

3. Test whether user manuals provide adequate guidelines in the following areas:

   - Complete description of the system.
   - Input instructions, including collection points and times to send updated information.
   - Reconciliation instructions.
   - Full listing of output reports, including sample formats.

4. Obtain work flows from the user manuals or managers showing data from the point-of-entry, through user processes, to final product.

   - Test the processes with users to determine if they know where the data is coming from, where it is going, and how it gets there.
   - Identify the points in which data adjustments occur.

- Identify the individuals accountable for contributing to data and reports. Compare information with the material acquired in the step immediately preceding this step.
- Test the preparation and reconciliation processes to verify the integrity of information.
- Determine if data adjustments are adequately documented.

5. Expand the sample by interviewing additional managers and experienced unit employees to determine their perceptions of MIS.

   - Discuss MIS principles of timeliness, accuracy, consistency, completeness, and relevancy.
   - Determine if the employees hold any significant perceptions that the MIS is ineffective.

6. If available, obtain samples of important recurring executive reports for the targeted MIS area(s). Test the following areas to determine if:

   - Information originates from the expected source business area.
   - Users of the information are the employees one would expect and the data is being used for correct purposes.
   - Distribution of the reports ultimately is supplied to all appropriate users.

7. Review a sample of audit workpapers relating to reports that disclosed material MIS weaknesses.

   - Review documents to determine if auditors tested MIS activities against policies or practices and processes.
   - Test to determine if documented findings support the audit scope and report comments.

www.ingramcontent.com/pod-product-compliance
Lightning Source LLC
Chambersburg PA
CBHW080806290526
45790CB00008B/3592